FROM COACH TO COACH

A Practical Guide to Coaching Youth Baseball

For Coaches of 7 and 8-year-old Ballplayers

By Kary R. Shumway

Copyright 2015 by Kary R. Shumway. All rights reserved.

The information in this book is meant to supplement, not replace, proper youth baseball training. Like any sport involving speed, equipment, balance and environmental factors, baseball poses some inherent risk. The author and publisher advise readers to take full responsibility for safety and know their limits. Before practicing the skills described in this book, be sure that your equipment is well maintained, and do not take risks beyond your level of experience, aptitude, training, and comfort level.

Please check out the full library of Coach to Coach Books, or drop a line to us at CoachToCoachBooks@gmail.com. Thank you for reading!

Table of Contents

Coach's Note. 5

An Overview of Rookies 6

Keep It Rookies Simple. 8

What to Expect 10

Season Checklist 12

Recruit Assistant Coaches 14

Safety & Fun. 15

Practice Drills 17

    The Baseball Field 17

    Running the Bases 18

    Throwing 19

    Fielding – Infield Drills 27

    Fielding – Catching a Thrown Ball. 37

    Hitting - Basics Before Batting 39

    Hitting the Baseball 42

Practice Plan Worksheets 51

    Overview of the Practice Plan Worksheets 51

Game Time 61

Odds & Ends of Coaching Rookies 63

Remember Why You Are Doing This. 65

Dedication. 66

Coach's Note

Many parents get into coaching Rookies because no one else will volunteer. Sound familiar? The team needs a coach and you decided to take on the job. It's not an easy decision, but it is the right one for you, your child and the team.

Like many parent coaches, I played baseball as a kid and loved the game. **However, playing the game and teaching it are two different things.** In fact, when I started my volunteer coaching "career", I hadn't given much thought as to the proper way to throw or catch a baseball in years, if ever.

So I bought books on baseball, attended coaching clinics, and talked to other coaches. Each year I learned a little more, figured out what worked (and what failed miserably) and eventually compiled a solid blueprint for how to coach and organize a team.

This coach's guide is a result of my personal experience - a simple, straightforward approach to organizing and coaching your seven and eight-year-olds.

I hope you find this information useful, whether you are just starting out, or like me, you've coached for several years and are looking for ways to improve.

An Overview of Rookies

The Rookies division of Cal Ripken youth baseball is for seven and eight-year-old kids. The objective of Rookies is to continue teaching basic baseball skills in a fun and supportive way. The skills learned in this division should build on the fundamentals the kids learned in Tee Ball. In Rookies, the games start to become somewhat competitive, as scores are kept and outs are recorded. Overall, the games are more formal than in Tee Ball.

Different leagues may have slightly different rules, but here are some Rookies game basics:

Scores are kept during the game, outs are recorded, and after three outs in an inning the kids change sides. Only 10 players are allowed in the field at once, and only 10 players can come up to bat in a given inning (unless the defensive team records 3 outs first). If a team has more than 10 players, there will be some kids who have to sit on the bench when the rest of the team is in the field. This introduces some new challenges, which are discussed later on.

The ball used in Rookies is usually the same soft ball used in Tee Ball. The ball is much softer than a regular baseball, and is usually made of rubber or a sponge material. The ball will usually indicate that it is an official "Tee Ball" or is a safety-training ball. Be careful to separate regular hard baseballs from your bucket of Tee Balls! *(Regular baseballs are hard and unforgiving when they are caught with a player's nose instead of the glove.)*

The batters and base runners must wear helmets. Even though the ball is softer than a regular baseball, it will hurt if it hits a player, so it's important to protect the noggin.

Great caution should be taken with baseball bats. Kids love to swing the bats and they rarely exercise caution when doing so. One of the first things you should do as a coach is establish rules about when it is OK to touch a baseball bat. No one touches a bat unless a coach is there with him or her. This way, the coach can be the eyes and ears to make sure no one is going to get hit.

Games and practices are generally kept short, 60 to 90 minutes at most. This time limit helps to preserve the sanity of the coaches, and matches up with the limited attention spans of the kids.

During games, coaches are encouraged to be in the field with the kids to provide instruction and guidance. However, unlike in Tee Ball, where the coaches can be anywhere (and everywhere) the Rookies division usually stipulates that the coaches remain in the outfield grass, and not in the infield area.

The coach will pitch to the batters, so the batting Tee is usually put away for the Rookies games. However, if a player is really struggling to hit a pitched ball, it's a good idea to have a batting Tee available for them to use.

Keep It Rookies Simple

In any baseball book or online search, you'll find hundreds of baseball drills readily available for use. The challenge is not finding the drills, but determining what will actually work in practices.

This coach's manual provides manageable, hands-on Rookies drills, and practice plans useful for teaching kids the fundamentals of the game.

Repetition is key. Learning a few key drills proficiently rather than limited exposure to dozens of different drills will help create the muscle memory necessary for improvement.

Be positive. No yelling. *Always Positive, Always Constructive.*

Be consistent. Develop routines so the kids know what to expect. Begin and end practices on time so the parents know what to expect.

Talk less, play more. You will have the full attention of your kids for about ten seconds. Provide a few simple instructions and then go play. Tell them, show them, and let them work it out.

Keep the players moving. The kids need constant action; rotating between stations, running, fielding, and hitting. Plan your practice with a "no standing around rule" to keep the kids engaged, exercising, and to avoid the dreaded phrase – "this is boring!"

Be patient. This one is the most difficult, and most important. Teaching the game, like learning the game, takes time and repetition.

Be yourself. You are there to have fun too.

Take charge. If you don't the kids will and it will be like Lord of the Flies on the baseball diamond. Use a whistle, a hand clap, or a key phrase to get the kids to snap to attention. Whatever device you use, be firm and in charge.

Involve older, experienced players in practices whenever possible. A high school baseball player at practices can make a world of difference. Younger kids look up to older kids, and most will give these "assistant coaches" their undivided attention.

Plan your practice in advance. Rookies practice plans may only take a few minutes, but make sure you arrive on the field with that plan in hand … or risk the fury of a dozen disorganized seven-year-olds!

What to Expect

What does a coach do and what is expected of you? Your responsibility may be limited to organizing practices and bringing the equipment bag to the game. You may also be responsible for coordinating player signups, league-certifying your coaches, scheduling umpires for game day, and a host of other logistical stuff.

As a new coach, you should ask a lot of questions. You may be taking over for a coach who is leaving or moving on to coach another team. In this case, ask the old coach questions so you can benefit from their knowledge. Otherwise, consult a league official.

The following questions should get you started.

Key Questions

- *What is the time commitment?*
- *Who do I contact with questions when I need help?*
- *Who coordinates player signups?*
- *What are the special rules of the game?*
- *Where are practices and games held?*
- *Who schedules field use?*
- *Where do I get player and parent contact information?*
- *How are team communications managed?*
- *Where do I get the equipment and uniforms?*
- *When does the season start and end?*
- *How many games are played? How many players are on my team?*

Many leagues offer coaching clinics before the season starts. These provide a great opportunity to meet with other coaches and to learn about the league. A league manual may also be available with answers to your questions.

As the coach, parents expect you to keep their kids safe and provide an opportunity to have a good time. Parents will expect you to be on time, be organized, and be in charge. And, just as important, players at the Rookie level will expect to be entertained outdoors while learning beginner baseball skills.

Season Checklist

Organization can make the difference between a successful season and one full of frustration. A baseball season checklist will help keep you on track. The season checklist serves as a reminder of what needs to be done and when. It is an organized list of 'to do' items which allows you to plan and delegate some of the work to parents or coaches who are willing to help out. People want to help and you need to lead them and provide clear direction.

To Do List	Date needed	Who is Responsible	Check when Completed
Stuff to get			
Baseball Equipment:			
Equipment Bag			
Helmets (5 or 6, different sizes)			
Bats (3 or 4, different sizes)			
Baseballs (new game balls)			
Baseballs (100+ for practices)			
Buckets (4 or 5 for practice stations)			
Batting T's			

Uniforms / Shirts			
Medical equipment:			
Ice Packs (keep 4 to 6 on hand)			
Medical kit (band aids, etc)			
Other:			
Clipboard, pen			
Scorebook			
Stuff to do			
Collect Parent and Player Contact Details			
Hold "Coaches Only" Meeting			
Hold Parent Meeting			
Follow-up with Letter to Parents			
Arrange for Practice Field Days/Times			
Find Volunteer Parent for Game Scorebook			
Schedule Umpires for Games			

Recruit Assistant Coaches

You will need, and want, some extra help to keep all the kids organized. While many parents do not want to be the "Coach" (that's why you have the job) they are usually willing to help out. Your job is to ask for help and provide direction when they agree to lend a hand.

Role of Assistant Coaches.

Work with kids on simple drills during practices.

Be a field presence during games to keep the kids alert and attentive.

Help bring baseball equipment to games.

Serve as substitute coach if you cannot make it to a game.

Availability of Assistant Coaches. Ask about work schedules or other commitments that may preclude a coach from being able to attend a practice or a game on a given day. This will help you set practice days and times, and ensure you will have enough help when you need it.

Coach the Coaches. You may find that your assistant coaches are unfamiliar with baseball fundamentals, let alone how to teach the game. First, familiarize yourself with the drills and sample practice plans. Next, review the drills with your assistant coaches, teaching them first. This will be good practice for you and your coaches, and will highlight areas that need enhanced instruction.

Safety & Fun

Being safe is a primary goal for this age level. Remember, the game of baseball requires the use of baseball bats - the kids swing the bats and occasionally throw them after they swing. So have a good plan in place before you allow your players to pick up a bat. Communicate with your assistant coaches and your players early and often – *no one touches a bat unless a coach is there.*

Prior to the first practice, make sure you have a fully stocked medical kit and plenty of cold packs. Let your coaches know where the kits are located. It's best to keep these items with the equipment bag so they are not left behind.

Keep the parent contact list safely on-hand, maybe including a copy in the medical kit, so you can contact them in case of an emergency. Your league will likely require parents to sign medical release forms, and provide an emergency contact in the event a parent is not available.

Bring on the fun! Baseball is a tough game requiring a lot of different motor skills and patience – two things that kids at this age are still developing. Work to introduce drills that teach skills in a fun way, using games. Try throwing drills that involve knocking over a milk jug, for example, or hitting drills with a home run derby, where a home run is a ball hit out of the infield.

Use legendary college basketball coach John Wooden's four laws of learning: demonstrate, imitate, correct, repeat. Kids don't always listen or understand the terms we use ("square up at the plate!" or "keep your eye on the ball!") but they can imitate us. Show the players what the drill looks like and what they are supposed to do and then have them imitate the drill. Correct any mistakes and have the kids repeat the drill.

And remember: ***Always Positive, Always Constructive.***

Practice Drills

The secret to a successful practice is to have a well thought-out plan, and plenty of help from parents or assistant coaches. The sample practice plans shown at the end of this chapter will help you with planning; it's up to you to recruit those assistant coaches and get them to help keep the kids organized.

As the saying goes, even the best-laid plans can go awry. Be flexible when you need to, and don't be afraid to change the plan if it just isn't working. Rome wasn't built in a day, and Tommy isn't going to learn to be a pro ballplayer in one 60-minute practice. It takes time and patience, good humor, and perspective to coach your Rookies team through a full baseball season. Do your best to plan and organize but enjoy the ride when the wheels come off, because they inevitably will.

Before we begin, here's a quick note about **keywords**. Kids do not retain a lot of instructions, but they will retain keywords. Where possible, use a keyword to name or describe the drill or skill you are working on.

For example, we use the term *Ready Position* to prompt the kids to take an athletic stance. This will help the kids associate the keyword with what they need to do or what's supposed to happen next. Keywords are used throughout the drills below.

THE BASEBALL FIELD

Practice Idea #1

Goal: Start by teaching the kids the basics of the baseball field and player positions. Most kids will have learned this in Tee Ball, but you may have a handful of kids who have never played the game before. Start with the basics.

Exercise: Gather the kids at home plate, and quiz them individually – "Where is first base? Where is second base?" and see how well they know the bases.

Homework: Have the kids sketch a picture of the baseball field, identifying 1st base, 2nd base, 3rd base and home plate. Have them write in the player positions as well and indicate where each player will be in the field. Many kids don't know which is right field and which is left field. The placement of the shortstop or second baseman can be tricky too. When I first ask kids to go play 2nd base, they instinctively run out there and stand right on top of the bag. Kids are very literal creatures.

RUNNING THE BASES

Practice Idea #2

Goal: Teach the kids how to properly run the bases.

Exercise: Run and Call Out the Name of the Bases. This exercise reinforces their understanding of the name and location of this base. Start by lining the kids up at home plate, and instruct them to run around the bases, making sure they touch each base. You can have them yell out the name of the base when they touch it, "First base!" "Second base!" and so on. Make sure they run fast, and touch each base.

To keep things orderly, have them line up at home plate, and have one player run first, when the player reaches first base and continues towards second base, have the next player start to run. This will help avoid collisions and keep the players spread out.

Practice Idea #3

Goal: Teach the kids to run fast to first base without stopping once they touch the bag.

Exercise: Run Through the Base. First base is the only base that the player can run past and not be tagged out by a fielder. This game is designed to teach the kids to run hard all the way to first, touch the base and keep running straight through first base.

After touching first base, the runner will then turn to her right (towards foul territory) and then return to stand on first base. They may not know exactly why they are doing this, but instructing them with the keywords, *Run Through the Base,* will establish this fundamental skill for when the games become competitive and outs are counted.

THROWING

Throwing a baseball is not a natural motion, and the coaches will need to spend a lot of time teaching some very basic throwing mechanics at this age level. This will be a slow process but will benefit the player for as long as they play the game.

Practice Idea #4

Goal: Teach the player to hold the baseball with a proper grip.

Exercise: There are two basic ways to hold the baseball – the four seam grip and the two seam grip. For the four seam grip, first, show the player the seams on the baseball. The index and middle finger of the throwing hand should grip the baseball across the wider portion of the seams on the ball. This is hard for kids with little hands, and most kids will need to use three fingers or their whole hand to grip the ball. However, an introduction to this grip is important early on, so it will be understood later when their hands are a little bigger.

The two seam grip is a little easier for kids with smaller hands. For this grip, the player will put their fingers along the narrower seams of the ball – these seams look kind of like railroad tracks.

Show the grips (pictures below) and have the kids practice holding and throwing the ball this way. If they just can't do it, let them use three fingers, but this will be a good introduction to the proper grip.

Homework: Have the kids take home a ball and practice these grips over and over. The more they grip the ball with two seams or four seams, the more natural it will feel.

The Four Seam Grip looks like this:

Photo: Four Seam Grip 1

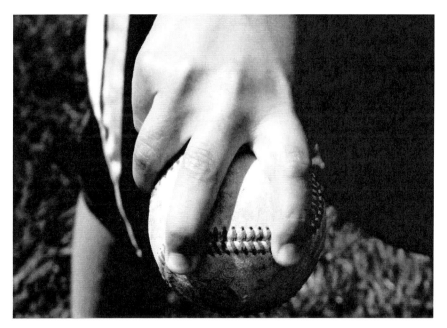

Photo: Four Seam Grip 2

The Two Seam Grip looks like this:

Photo: Two Seam Grip 1

Photo: Two Seam Grip 2

Photo: Two Seam Grip 3

Practice Idea #5

Goal: Teach the player the correct throwing motion.

Exercise: Point, Step, and Throw. To align properly for the throw, have the player <u>point</u> the glove (and left hip, if a right-handed thrower) toward the target. Next, have him step towards the target with the left leg, shifting the weight to the front foot as they begin the throwing motion with their arm. Have the player maintain the pointing of the glove towards the target during the initial throwing movement. This will keep the player from leading the throw with the chest, and opening up the body too early. The instructions here assume a right-handed thrower, just reverse these for a lefty.

Homework: Practice the *Point, Step and Throw* at home. Make 25 good throws to mom or dad.

Photo: Point

Photo: Step

Photo: Throw

Practice Idea #6

Goal: Teach the player to follow through on their throw.

Exercise: The Big Finish. This next drill emphasizes the follow through of the throw, or the Big Finish. In order to promote a good, long follow through, have the kids finish the throw with their throwing hand grazing their left knee (outside knee). This will force them to extend the arm at the finish. You can have the kids 'freeze' in the *Big Finish* to show them where their hand/arm should finish. The final picture in the *Point, Step and Throw series* above shows the player in the *Big Finish* pose.

Practice Idea #7

Goal: Work on throwing accuracy by having the players throw at a target.

Exercise: Hit the Cones. Line up two cones near the backstop, about 10 feet apart. Make two lines with your players, the two lines also 10 feet apart, and in line with the cones. Position a coach a few feet away from each cone. When the coach tells them to start, have each player in each line throw the ball at the cone, then go to the back of the line and the next player throws. Give each player in each line three or four throws, and count which line knocked over the most cones.

This game can quickly descend into mayhem, with kids firing baseballs all over the place. To keep things organized, tell the kids they must use a proper *Point, Step, and Throw* with each throw. If a player does not follow this rule, they won't be credited with any cones they knock down. The kids hate that, but it is an effective way to get them to slow down and concentrate on making a proper throw.

Practice Idea #8

Goal: Teach the players to warm up with a controlled game of catch.

Exercise: Playing Catch (without chaos). Playing catch is one of the basics of baseball, yet it is a difficult exercise with seven- and eight-year-old players who are not proficient at either throwing or catching.

When I first started coaching, we would have the kids start off practice with a game of catch. The result was terrifying: Balls flying everywhere, kids spread out randomly in the field, and the kids lost track of their throwing partner so they would fling the ball at the first player they saw. I quickly learned that we need to provide specific instructions to keep the game of catch a bit more organized.

Start by showing the kids what a game of catch should look like; one coach throws to another, they catch it and throw it back. Make note of the fact that they are throwing to each other, and not launching the baseball ten feet over the other person's head. To keep the players lined up properly, have one coach stand on the right field foul line and the other coach stand about 15 feet away.

Show the players that if a ball is not caught and the player has to run to retrieve the ball, the player must return to his original throwing spot to resume play. The players must maintain their original throwing location - this helps to keep the kids in neat rows, and lined up across from their partner. If you have cones, you can make two rows, placing a cone where each player should stand. Tell the kids they must return to their cone prior to throwing the ball to their partner.

Homework: Play catch at home with mom or dad and make 25-50 good throws and catches.

FIELDING – INFIELD DRILLS

Practice Idea #9

Goal: Teach the kids to be ready to field the ball when they are on defense.

Exercise: Ready Position. This keyword is used a lot, and at every age level in baseball. There is a lot of down time for kids playing in the field, and a lot of time for the kids to lose focus and interest in the game. *Ready Position* reminds the kids to get ready and pay attention. When the ball is being pitched to the batter, the fielders should be in an 'athletic stance' with legs about shoulder width apart, knees slightly bent, hands low and ready to field the ball.

In between pitches, or when there is a pause in the game, the kids on defense can relax and don't need to remain frozen in the *Ready Position* . Teach them when they need to be attentive, and when they can wave to Grandpa sitting in the stands, or check out the flock of geese that is flying overhead.

Practice Idea #10

Goal: Teach the kids to use two hands when fielding the baseball.

Exercise: Alligator Trap. This keyword instructs the kids to use their throwing hand to trap the ball in the glove. Show the kids how the top hand "chomps down" on the bottom glove hand resembles an Alligator. Coaches usually instruct the kids: "use two hands!" But *Alligator Trap* is a little more fun and kids seem to understand it.

We also say that the *Alligator Trap* saves your nose, as your top hand (throwing hand) will trap down on the ball, and in the case of a bad hop, the ball will hit your hand rather than your face. Use this keyword when drilling on ground balls so kids learn to use that throwing hand to trap the ball. The added benefit of *Alligator Trap* is that by using the throwing hand in this way, the hand is in position to grab the ball and then make a good throw to first base.

Photo: Alligator Trap 1

Photo: Alligator Trap with Ball

Practice Idea #11

Goal: Teach the kids how to properly field the baseball with soft hands.

Exercise: Soft Hands. Have the kids drop the gloves and give them slow rollers to field with their bare hands. This will have them develop a feel for softly scooping up the ball and involving both hands.

Soft Hands is used to describe making a smooth play on the ball. Kids may want to stab at the ball, but *Soft Hands* drills them on techniques to use a little 'give' when receiving the ball and absorb the ball into the belly.

Practice Idea #12

Goal: Work on the Alligator Trap and Soft Hands drills together.

Exercise: No Glove. To work on *Soft Hands* and using two hands to field a ball, have the kids drop the gloves and give them slow rollers to field with their bare hands. This will have them develop a feel for softly scooping up the ball and involving both hands.

Photo: Soft Hands, No Glove

Practice Idea #13

Goal: Teach the kids to look at the target when throwing the baseball.

Exercise: Look at the Target. When making the throw, ensure kids are looking at their target. This seems obvious but the kids may be rushing to field the ball, they may bobble it, then they just launch the throw in whatever direction they may be facing at the time. Remind them often to *Look at the Target*. Then ensure they are using the proper throwing mechanics you've worked on above.

Practice Idea #14

Goal: Teach the player to move quickly toward a rolling baseball.

Exercise: Slow Rollers. This drill works on an aggressive move to the ball. Many times a slow ground ball is hit, and the infielder gets in the *Ready Position* and waits - and waits - for the ball to get to them. Eventually the ball reaches the fielder, but the batter might be standing on second base with a double by the time the ball gets to the infielder. Have the kids work on recognizing when the ball is rolling slowly they should charge the ball, field it and make a throw.

Photo: Slow Roller 1

Photo: Slow Roller 2

Practice Idea #15

Goal: Teach the player gain momentum and power when throwing the baseball.

Exercise: Shuffle step before the throw. Roll a ground ball to the player, and have them field the ball. Before they throw the ball to first base, or back to the coach, have them take two *Shuffle Steps* towards their target. *Shuffle Steps* involve having the player step towards the target with the front foot, and then shuffle or drag the front foot. The player will be shuffling with the front shoulder (throwing shoulder) pointing to the target. Have the player shuffle twice towards the target and release the throw. This takes a little time to get the foot and body coordination down, but it promotes a good strong throw.

Photo: Shuffle Step 1

Photo: Shuffle Step 2

Practice Idea #16

Goal: Teach the player how to make an underhand toss instead of overhand throw

Exercise: Underhand Toss. This drill is good for second basemen and shortstops primarily, when working on flips to second base for a force out. For many kids this is a tough play, because it is a 'subtle' toss play. Many kids want to fling the ball underhanded, sending the ball too fast for the receiving player to make the catch.

Have the player field a ground ball and then make the *Underhand Toss* to the player standing on second base. The *Underhand Toss* is performed by the player fielding the ball, who then makes a short shuffle towards the bag to build momentum with the throwing hand (or tossing hand) extended long and towards the target. The ball is equally pushed and tossed to the receiver. The toss ends with the throwing fingers extended towards the target. This drill is challenging as it takes 'touch' and 'finesse' to find the right speed of the toss.

Photo: Underhand Toss 1

Photo: Underhand Toss 2

FIELDING – CATCHING A THROWN BALL

Many players at this age have difficulty catching a thrown ball, let alone a pop up. Therefore you should concentrate most of your games on using ground balls. However, with a coach and player, you can use the practice ideas below to work on the basics of catching safety balls.

Practice Idea #17

Goal: Work on the proper glove position for catching a thrown baseball.

Exercise: Thumbs Up / Thumbs Down. These keywords indicate how a player should catch a ball depending on the height of the thrown ball. If the throw is above the waist, the player should catch the ball with Thumbs Up – the glove should be pointed up. If the ball is below the waist, Thumbs Down, glove pointed down. Practice soft, underhand tosses and call out to the player, "Thumps Up" or "Thumbs Down" depending on the height of the toss.

Homework: Have the kids practice this drill at home with mom or dad for 15 minutes before the next game. This skill takes a lot of repetition before it becomes instinctual. I've seen kids continue to try and catch a ball that is up around their eyeballs with a Thumbs Down technique. This is remarkably hard to do, but it does happen.

Photo: Thumbs Up Catching

Photo: Thumbs Down Catching

Practice Idea #18

Goal: Work on having the players catch fly balls using soft tennis balls.

Exercise: Tennis ball pop ups. Tennis balls are lighter and softer than the safety balls, so they won't hurt as much when a player catches one off the nose. This will allow the players and coaches to practice catching pop ups without fear of injury.

With a bucket of tennis balls, the coach stands about 20 feet from the player. The coach then makes underhand tosses of the tennis ball to the player, throwing the ball 10 to 15 feet in the air for the player to catch. If the player is proficient, the coach can throw the ball higher in the air. If the player is struggling, make the tosses lower and easier to catch.

Homework: Practice tennis ball pop ups at home with mom or dad. When I was a kid my dad would come home from work and throw us pop flies for hours. I count these among some of my best memories from childhood. So, practice at home and not only will you learn to catch better, but also you'll make a lasting memory with dear old dad (or mom).

HITTING - BASICS BEFORE BATTING

Kids love to hit baseballs. You can't blame them, as it is a lot of fun. However, before they start hacking away it is important to quickly cover the basics: choosing the right sized bat, proper grip of the bat, and position at the plate.

Choosing the right sized bat. For seven and eight year old Rookie players, the bat length should be 24" to 26" inches. All the bats are pretty light these days, so weight shouldn't be an issue. However, there is always one kid who brings a huge wooden bat to practice or games and insists on hitting with it. Unless the kids can hit like Ted Williams, put the wooden bat away and stick with nice, lightweight aluminum bat.

Practice Idea #19

Goal: Teach the player to grip the baseball bat properly.

Exercise: Hands together. The most common issue with kids gripping the bat is that their hands are apart. Show the player how to hold the bat, with hands together. Next, have them line up the knuckles on each hand. The 2nd knuckles of the top hand should line up with the 3rd knuckles on the bottom hand. Count those knuckles down from your fingertip: 1st knuckle, 2nd knuckle, then 3rd knuckle and you've got it. This is one of those skills you don't think about much as an adult, you just grab a bat and you've usually got the proper grip. Kids, however, come up with all kinds of wacky grips in order to hold a bat. It's useful to take the time to show them a proper grip.

Homework: Have the kids practice their grip at home. Make the proper grip, put the bat down and then and re-grip the bat. This is similar to the proper grip of the baseball. If they do it over and over it will eventually become a natural motion.

Photo: Proper Grip of Bat

Practice Idea #20

Goal: Teach the player to take the proper position at the plate when batting.

Exercise: Position at the Plate. When batting, where the player stands in relation to the batting Tee will depend on the player's size, reach, and ability. To start, have the player step into the batters box, set their feet, and take a few practice swings. The coach can then have the player move closer or further away from the Tee as appropriate for the player to make good contact. Once the proper position is established, the coach should draw a line in the dirt to indicate where the player should stand. Have the player step away from the batting Tee, and then re-take the proper position at the plate putting their *Toes on the Line*. Repeat this so the kids get a feel for where they should stand in relation to the Tee and to home plate.

The real key when positioning at the plate is that the kids remember to actually do it when they get in the batter's box. Work with them on a routine, this will help them focus on their proper *Position* and it will get them in the right frame of mind for hitting.

Photo: Position at the Plate

HITTING THE BASEBALL

"I think without question the hardest single thing to do in sport is to hit a baseball". – Ted Williams

Hitting a round ball with a rounded bat is tough to do. However, hitting a baseball solidly is one of the more enjoyable experiences here on planet earth, so it is worth the trouble to figure out how to do it properly.

To boil it down, there are only three steps to hitting the baseball: Load, Contact, and Finish.

These are also good keywords to use in each of the hitting drills described below. "Load" refers to the weight shift the player makes to the back foot, prior to swinging. This "Loads" the swing, and prepares the player to "Explode" forward into the pitch.

Think of *loading* the swing like the pulling back on a slingshot. "Contact" simply refers to the moment of hitting the baseball. During "Contact" the player's eyes should be on the ball (not closed, or looking up at the sky), and they should be driving or shifting their weight forward. The "Finish", refers to the completion of a swing, where the player makes a good follow through and transfer of weight to the front foot.

In the Rookies division, the Tee is put away for games and the coach pitches the ball to the batter. The goal is to make nice easy throws that the player can hit. Because of the height difference between coach (pitcher) and player (batter), I recommend that you kneel on one knee when pitching to the kids. This changes the angle of the throw, and allows for more consistent pitches at the height of the batter. Alternatively, you can flip over a 5 gallon bucket, and pitch from a seated position. Practice both methods and see which works best.

Some leagues use a pitching machine in place of the coaches. The machines usually deliver more consistent pitches but require the coach to learn how to set up the machine and adjust it for different pitch heights and speeds to match the player's height and ability.

Practice Idea #21

Goal: Teach the player how to shift their weight back and then forward to create power in their swing.

Exercise: Load and Explode. In order to create power, the player must learn how to shift their weight back and then forward during the swing. Similar to making a shuffle step before a throw, the weight shift creates momentum and power for the batter.

To demonstrate the feeling of the weight shift, have the player stand flat-footed and throw a punch in the air. They will find that the punch is ineffective, and not very powerful. Now have them shift their weight to their right foot as they pull their right arm back to throw the punch. Next, have them shift their weight forward to their left foot as they are throwing the punch. They will find they have much more force on the punch. This is the same concept as *Loading* the swing. The player must *Load* (shift weight back), and then *Explode* (shift weight forward) as they make the swing.

For this drill, have the player take their *Position at the Plate*, and instruct them to *Load* their swing, with a shifting of their weight to the back foot. Next, have them *Explode* into the swing with a shifting of weight to the front foot. Repeat this several times so the player can get a feel for the shifting of weight from back to front during the swing.

Photo: Hitting Load Step

Photo: Hitting Load Step 2

Photo: Hitting Explode

Practice Idea #22

Goal: Teach the player to make a full swing of the baseball bat.

Exercise: Squish the Bug. This drill reinforces the weight shift from back foot to front foot during the swing. Using a batting Tee, have the player take several full swings. As the player finishes their swing they should pivot, or twist, their back foot. This promotes a good follow through, and transfer of weight from back to front foot. The key words *Squish the Bug* gives the player a visual to think about as they pivot their back foot, and squish the imaginary bug.

Photo: Squish the Bug

Practice Idea #23

Goal: Teach the player to make consistent, solid contact with the baseball off the batting Tee.

Exercise: Contact. This is where the bat meets the ball. Making good contact with the baseball requires hand-eye coordination, proper swing mechanics and a lot of practice.

Start by having the player hit the ball off the batting Tee into a net. They will likely moan and groan about this, because they are "not in Tee Ball anymore." You can remind them that Major League ballplayers use batting Tees in practice all the time to work on their swing, so they are not just for little kids.

Have the player take several swings using the batting Tee until they can make consistent solid contact with the baseball. Note whether they are using *Load and Explode* during the swing to properly shift their weight.

If they are having trouble making good contact check their *Position at the Plate* and ensure they are standing the proper distance from the Tee. Watch their head position as they make the swing – kids have a tendency to swing hard and turn their head away from the ball. They usually want to see where the ball goes, so they jump the gun and turn their head early in anticipation of great hit.

Meanwhile, the ball is still sitting on the batting Tee. Remind them to keep their head down and eyes watching the ball through contact. One trick to keep the head down is to instruct them to <u>continue</u> looking at the batting Tee after contact of the baseball.

Photo: Hitting Load Step Contact

Practice Idea #24

Goal: Teach the player to make consistent, solid contact with the baseball pitched by the coach.

Exercise: Contact, part 2. Once the player can make consistent contact with the baseball on the batting Tee, it's time to have the coach pitch batting practice. The goal is for the player to take what they learned on the batting Tee and use those skills to hit a pitched baseball.

Start by having the player take the proper *Position at the Plate*, and have the coach make slow pitches to the player. If they are having trouble hitting the ball, have them step away from the plate and relax for a few seconds.

Don't let the kids get discouraged if they don't hit the ball consistently. As Ted Williams said, *"Hitting a baseball is one of the toughest things to do in all of sports"*. Keep practicing and rotating the kids back to the batting Tee to work on their hand-eye coordination.

Practice Idea #25

Goal: Teach the player to make a controlled swing with a full follow through.

Exercise: Photo Finish. Have the player make a full swing, and hold the finish at the conclusion of the swing. Hopefully, the player will still be upright and balanced when they finish the swing. To reinforce control and balance, have the kids *Pose* at the finish of the swing as though someone were taking their picture. The kids will usually goof around with this one, but if they are not laying flat on the ground after the swing, you can consider this an accomplishment.

As they get older and have more body control, the *Photo Finish* will help them remember to swing hard and under control.

Photo: Photo Finish

Practice Plan Worksheets

The worksheets that follow serve as one-page summaries of your practice plan. This methodology will keep you organized and allow you to easily communicate the practice plan to your coaches. You can also share worksheets with parents so kids can work on drills at home with mom or dad.

OVERVIEW OF THE PRACTICE PLAN WORKSHEETS

The basics: *Write down the practice day, location, starting time, and ending time.* Don't forget to stick to the one-hour rule: no practices longer than an hour. In addition to preserving the sanity of the coaches, the one-hour rule makes it easy for parents to drop their kids off and pick them back up on time.

The pre-practice routine. When kids arrive at practice, they should immediately have a job to do. Usually, this job involves gathering into a group while a coach leads stretching exercises, jumping jacks, and a jog around the outfield. Without a specific routine upon arrival, they will start rooting through the equipment bag, grabbing bats and balls, and creating mayhem. It is not pretty and its not how you want to start practice. As the kids warm up with one coach, the other coaches can set up the stations for the planned drills.

Begin practices with an explanation of what you will work on. Start off with a very brief team meeting – no longer than two or three minutes. This can be done after all the kids have arrived and have completed their pre-practice routine (running, stretching, etc). For the team meeting, gather into a circle and have the kids *Take a Knee* by kneeling on one knee. You can tell them this is what the big league ball players do. *Taking a Knee* also keeps them from lying down, rolling around and tackling one another.

Briefly explain what you will work on that day and what is expected of them. For example: "Today in our baseball practice we will learn about the *Ready Position* when playing in the field. We will learn how to run to first base really fast and *Run Through the Bag*. We will hit baseballs off of the Tee and will learn to take the proper *Position at the Plate*."

The introduction to each practice and game should include the keywords for the drills you will be practicing – *Ready Position, Run Through the Bag,* and *Position at the Plate*. The kids won't understand these at first, but with repetition, the keywords start to be meaningful baseball commands for both players and coaches.

Remind the kids that they are baseball players. Baseball players are good listeners and give their best effort on every play, and this is what the coaches expect to see today. Baseball players remember to bring their glove and their baseball hat to practice, they play hard, and are respectful of their teammates and coaches. And mostly, baseball players get to have a lot of fun.

The Baseball Stations. Outline the different drills to be worked on during practice and the different 'stations' or locations to perform the drills. This set-up depends on how many skills you want to work on, how many coaches and players are involved, and how much of the baseball field you can work with.

For example, you may have twelve kids, three coaches, and want to cover three different drills during your practice. Therefore, you can do a little math and break the kids into three groups of four kids each with each coach in charge of a station. Your three skills could be *Ready Position, Run*

Through the Bag, and *Position at the Plate*. One coach would then take four players to the infield station and work on *Ready Position*. Another coach would take four players to home plate and work on running to first base for *Run Through the Bag*. The third coach would take four players to left field where a net is set up to work on *Position at the Plate*. The kids would each spend 5 or 10 minutes at each station, and then rotate to the next station.

As you sketch out the practice plan, you may run into scenarios where two or more drills need to occur at the same spot on the field. In the previous example, it would be best to have the kids work on *Position at the Plate* at the actual home plate, but this would interfere with the kids who are starting at home plate and learning to run fast to first base - *Run Through the Bag*. I've found that moving drills to the outfield works just fine and provides proper spacing and separation so the kids aren't crashing into each other.

End practice with a talk about what you have learned that day. I like to ask the kids what they liked about practice first and then what they learned. I usually do it in this order because the question 'what did you learn today?' usually stumps them or possibly reminds them of the question they get from their parents when they get home from school.

When I ask, "what did you like today?" they usually pipe up with things they thought were fun. From there, you can remind them that they actually learned about *Ready Position*, how to *Run Through the Bag*, and how to take the proper *Position at the Plate*.

Rookies Practice Plan Worksheet # 1
Monday 6pm-7pm
Next Practice: Saturday 9am-10am
Pre-practice Routine: With Coach, stretches, jumping jacks, then two laps around the field.
Team meeting: Gather the kids at home plate and have them take a knee (Explain drills and goals for today's practice: **"Ready Position"**, **"Run Through the Bag"** and **"Position at the Plate"**. Quick description of each baseball skill that we will work on. Reminder that we are baseball players, we are good listeners, we give our best effort on every play, we are good teammates, and we have fun!
Station Work (divide into three groups, rotate kids through stations every 5-10 minutes)
Station 1: Ready Position. In the Infield.
Players form a line near 2nd base. Coach shows the players the *Ready Position* – feet apart, knees bent, eyes on the batter, glove in a position ready to field the ball. Coach instructs the players to get into *Ready Position* then roll the ball to the player. Player fields the ball and rolls back to the Coach.
Station 2: Run Through the Bag. At home plate.

Players line up at home plate.

When instructed by the coach, one player at a time runs to first base, run fast, touch the base.

Repeat two or three times, telling the kids to run hard through the bag – touch the base and keep running fast, to ensure they don't slow down prior to reaching the base.

Next, show the players how to touch first base, continue running and make a right hand turn into foul territory – the area to the right of first base (or usually the area where mom and dad are sitting in the stands).

When instructed by the coach, one player at time runs through the bag, then turns to foul territory. Repeat two or three times for each player.

Station 3: Position at the Plate. In the Outfield.

Prior to practice coach will have set up a net in the outfield. The players will use the batting tee and hit balls into the net after learning how to take the correct "Position at the Plate".

Each player must wear a helmet, only one bat is allowed, and the coach will carry it, until the drill is ready to begin

The batting tee will be setup just in front of the net. The coach will demonstrate how to take the *Position at the Plate.*

Each player in turn will take the proper *Position at the Plate*, hit the ball off the tee into the net.

The key with this drill is getting the kids to remember to check their feet, see where they need to be in relation to the batting tee, and to do this consistently. Have them take their position, then step away from the tee and see if they can reset themselves properly.

End of practice meeting: Ask the kids what they liked today. What should we work on next time? Ask what they learned today. Review the keywords and drills: "**Ready Position**", "**Run Through the Bag**", and "**Position at the Plate.**"

Rookies Practice Plan Worksheet # 2

Saturday 9am-10am

Next Practice: Wednesday 5pm-6pm

Pre-practice Routine: With Coach, stretches, jumping jacks. Five minutes of controlled game of catch with a partner. Then two laps around the field.

Team meeting: Gather the kids at home plate and have them take a knee. Explain drills and goals for today's practice: **"Point, Step and Throw"**, **"Squish the Bug"**, and **"Hit the Cones game"**. Quick description of each baseball skill that we will work on. Reminder that we are baseball players, we are good listeners, we give our best effort on every play, we are good teammates, and we have fun!
Station Work Divide into two groups, have kids rotate stations after 10-15 minutes
Station 1: Point, Step and Throw. The first group works on throwing drill in the Infield.
Line up the players along the first base line

Coach shows the players how to point towards the target with their glove hand and left hip (for right hand thrower), then step with their left foot towards the target and throw.

Players then take turns throwing to the coach, repeating the *Point, Step and Throw* movements. |
| **Station 2: Squish the bug**. Second group works on hitting in the Outfield. |
| Prior to practice a coach will set up a batting Tee and net in the outfield

The kids will practice hitting off the Tee into the net, and work on *Squish the Bug*.

Coach demonstrates for the players how to swing and pivot on the back foot to squish the imaginary bug.

Coach controls the bats, players must wear a helmet when hitting |

Station 3: Hit the cones game. All players at home plate.

Coach sets two orange cones near the backstop, and lines the players up into two groups about 15 feet apart near home plate and facing the backstop.

Coach will explain that the each player in turn will throw the ball and attempt to knock over their cone. Their team will get one point every time they knock over a cone, but they must use the proper throwing technique, *Point, Step, and Throw* or the point will not count.

After the player throws he or she will then go to the back of the line. Coaches will call out the points, and remind players of proper throwing steps.

End of practice meeting: Ask the kids what they liked today. What should we work on next time? Ask what they learned today. Review the keywords and drills: "**Point, Step, Throw**", and "**Squish the Bug**".

Rookies Practice Plan Worksheet # 3

Saturday 9am-10am

Next Practice: Wednesday 5pm-6pm

Pre-practice Routine: With Coach, stretches, jumping jacks, then two laps around the field

Team meeting: Gather the kids at home plate and have them take a knee. Explain drills and goals for today's practice: **"Thumbs up, Thumbs Down", "Soft hands",** and **"Photo Finish".** Quick description of each baseball skill that we will work on. Reminder that we are baseball players, we are good listeners, give our best effort on every play, are good teammates, and have fun!

Station Work Divide into two groups, have kids rotate stations after 10-15 minutes

Station 1: Thumbs up, Thumbs down. The first group works on catching in the outfield.

Line up kids in the outfield. If you have enough coaches, divide this group in two and have the second group line up about twenty feet away in the outfield.

Coach explains how baseball players catch a ball above their waist with *Thumbs Up* and a catch a ball below their waist with *Thumbs Down*.

Coach demonstrates the drill by making a soft underhand toss to another coach above the waist, then below the waist. The receiving coach will show the players how the Thumbs of both hands should be pointing Up to catch the ball above the waist, and down to catch the ball below the waist.

Repeat the drill by making soft underhand tosses to each player.

Station 2: Soft hands. The second group works on fielding in the infield.

Line up kids near second base. If you have enough coaches, divide this group in two and have the second group line up near first base allowing each player to get more chances to field the ball.

Coach explains that baseball players first learn to field ground balls with bare hands. This improves fielding skills by getting both hands involved in the play, and teaches Soft Hands to gently receive the ground ball.

Coach demonstrates the drill by rolling the ball to another coach. The fielding coach begins in *Ready Position,* then softly scoops the ground ball with two hands, and rolls the ball back to the coach.

Repeat the drill by rolling soft ground balls to the players.

Station 3: Photo Finish. All players work on batting. Half the players at Home plate, the other half in the outfield hitting off Tee into a net.

Coach demonstrates how to swing the bat, and maintain a balanced finish.

Have each player make a good full swing and *Pose* at the end of the swing as though someone was taking his or her picture. During their *Pose* the player should have completed their swing and be upright, and balanced.

Scrimmage game. Divide players into two teams and play a one-inning scrimmage game. All players get up to bat and then the teams change side. Coaches may stop play and give instructions to players.

End of practice meeting: Ask the kids what they liked today. What should we work on next time? Ask what they learned today. Review the Key Words and drills: **"Thumbs Up, Thumbs Down", "Soft Hands",** and **"Photo Finish".**

Game Time

Game time is exciting for the kids, coaches and parents. The kids get to wear their uniforms and look like real ballplayers. (Even if the uniform is only a t-shirt, it's still pretty cool.) The coaches are anxious and hopeful that their players will remember at least some of their new skills. Parents are excited and eager to see their little guys perform on the field, as this may be the first 'organized' sport that any of them have played. Game time is a big day for everyone involved with the Rookies team.

Your role during the games is to keep the kids safe, organized and having fun. Ideally, they'll also be working on their newly learned baseball skills. As with practices, you will need a game time routine to keep things running smoothly. Below are a few simple guidelines I have used with our players:

A reminder that we are baseball players, we are good listeners, we try our best on every play, and we respect our teammates, coaches and the other team.

All players will be on the bench or in the dugout when our team is at bat.

When waiting for your turn to hit, no player will touch a bat unless a coach is with them.

The Game Lineup sheet is a tool I've used over the years to write down the batting order and positions the kids will play in the field. In Rookies, this is more helpful for the coaches to make sure everyone gets to bat, in order, and plays different positions in the field – a simple way to keep track.

The Game Lineup sheet may also help you avoid the barrage of questions from the kids – "when do I get up to bat?" or "can I play first base?" If the kids can find their name on the sheet, they can answer this question for themselves and save you from hearing these questions a dozen times each inning.

Give your players a chance to play different positions each inning. The game lineup sheet will help ensure you rotate your players around, so they don't end up in right field the whole game, bored out of their mind.

Game Lineup Sheet (Example)

Batting and Fielding Lineup								
Our Team:	Blue Jays		Vs. Team:		Cardinals	Date:	June 1st	
Position they will play in the field								
Batting Order	Player Name	Player Jersey #	1st Inning	2nd Inning	3rd Inning	4th Inning	5th Inning	6th Inning
1	Tommy		1B	1B	P	P	1B	P
2	Nick		P	P	1B	3B	P	1B
3	John		C	C	C	C	C	C
4	Andrew		SS	2B	SS	CF	2B	SS
5	Martin		3B	3B	3B	1B	3B	3B
6	Samantha		LF	Bench	2B	LF	SS	LF
7	Timmy		2B	CF	Bench	2B	CF	2B
8	Michael		CF	SS	Bench	SS	Bench	CF
9	Ed		RF	Bench	LF	RF	Bench	LF
10	Jason		Bench	RF	CF	Bench	RF	Bench
11	Spencer		Bench	LF	RF	Bench	LF	Bench

Odds & Ends of Coaching Rookies

Coaching is teaching. Coaching baseball with a group of seven- and eight-year-olds can be rewarding, challenging, maddening and fulfilling all at the same time. One thing I've learned is that it takes a long time to develop the skills to play baseball and therefore teaching the game will take quite a bit of patience, but more importantly it will take *perspective*.

I like to focus on the things that are achievable and within the control of the kids – being good listeners, being respectful of players and coaches, and giving their best effort on every play (or most every play). These are the indicators of success, not how quickly a player learns to catch a fly ball or swing a bat. Learning baseball skills takes time but if the kids are trying their best and being good teammates, ultimately that is an accomplishment you can be proud of.

Coaching kids with behavior issues. Unfortunately, not all seven- and eight-year-old kids are well behaved, respectful and able to follow instructions. Sometimes you'll get a player or two that is particularly difficult to deal with and very disruptive to practices and games. If you find yourself in this situation, the first approach is to coach the kids about respectful behavior. Remind them what is expected of them. If this doesn't work, involve the parents, determine what you're dealing with, and get advice on how to handle the child. If all else fails, run them until they are too tired to disrupt the practice.

Dealing with difficult parents. Hopefully you won't have to experience this at the Rookies level. Difficulties usually arise when the kids get older and games become more competitive. However, if issues with parents arise, communication usually works. Talk to the parents and listen to their side of the story. Find out what is really going on. This takes time, something you probably don't have, but making the effort to talk to the difficult mom or dad often helps solve the problem.

Dealing with difficult assistant coaches. You need assistant coaches, but you will also have situations where coaching styles, personalities and/or approaches to situations will clash. If this happens, refer back to your coaching philosophy, and the pre-season coaches meeting. Talk with the difficult coach and listen to them. Sometimes a simple conversation will solve the problem, other times you may need to get help from a league official.

Remember Why You Are Doing This

There will be times during the season when you feel you have made a mistake by agreeing to be the coach. The kids aren't listening to instructions, they are goofing around, and it seems anything you try fails miserably. On these days it's helpful to remind yourself of your goal – why do you want to be a coach? Find your own reason, your own philosophy or motto, and remember it when times get tough.

I coach because I love the game of baseball and I love my son. My goal is to teach the game to the best of my ability and share this experience with my boy. This simple philosophy has sustained me through the many challenges of the youth baseball season.

From Coach to Coach, I wish you a successful and enjoyable season. Remember to have fun and enjoy the ups and downs that come from coaching a wild pack of Rookie players. The memories made here will last a lifetime.

Dedication

Everything I know about coaching baseball has come from the generous support and training I received from others who were willing to share their time and knowledge with me. Early on, I was the player, learning from my coach. And later, I was the coach, learning from the expertise of the coaches around me. No one learns anything without the help of amazing people along the way and I have been extremely fortunate to have learned from some of the best.

I want to say thank you to the many coaches who have helped me on my youth baseball coaching journey. First, my dad, who taught me to practice, work hard, play the game fair, and above all, have fun. Thank you to my youth baseball coach Bill Kosloski, who believed in me at a time when I wasn't sure I believed in myself. It meant everything to me and I will never forget it.

Thank you to my fellow coaches at the ConVal Cal Ripken league in New Hampshire: Steve Coty, Matt Harris, Luc Shippee, Paul Faber, Scott Daniels, Phil Dodge, Ed Suchocki, Gregg Fletcher, Rich Scheinblum, Paul McGrath, Scott Buffum, Scott Liljeberg, Greg Kriebel, Doug Davie, Scott Jaynes, Greg Blake, Kevin Proctor, and Chris Gallagher.

This book would not have been possible without the support, encouragement, time and effort from Sarah Kossayda, Sara Strube, and Oliver Strube from Abel Twitchell collective. Teammates are essential in baseball, and in completing a project like this. I could not have done it without you.

Thank you to Jenny Green who took many of the photos in the book. The good ones are hers. The less good ones are mine. You will be able to tell the difference. If you want great photos, drop Jenny a line at jenverde@comcast.net.

Most importantly, I want to thank my beautiful family: My loving and patient wife, who would wake up in the middle of the night wondering why I wasn't in bed ("I'm still typing!"). And my beautiful children, Max and Abigail who are the most amazing and wonderful things that I have ever laid eyes on.

I wouldn't be coaching if it weren't for my son. And I certainly wouldn't be writing a guide book about coaching. Max, even though you like soccer more than baseball, this book is dedicated to you.

January 2015

Thank you for reading From Coach to Coach. If you are interested in checking out the other books in the series please visit us at CoachToCoachBooks.com or click here for the full library of books.

Books in the From Coach to Coach youth baseball series:

From Coach to Coach, Lessons Learned Coaching Youth Baseball

From Coach to Coach, A Practical Guide to Coaching Youth Baseball, For Tee Ball Coaches

From Coach to Coach, A Practical Guide to Coaching Youth Baseball, For Coaches of 7 and 8 year-old Ballplayers

From Coach to Coach, A Practical Guide to Coaching Youth Baseball, For Coaches of 9 and 10 year-old Ballplayers

From Coach to Coach, A Practical Guide to Coaching Youth Baseball, For Coaches of 11 and 12 year-old Ballplayers

Manufactured by Amazon.ca
Acheson, AB